Killing Suicide

Dave Bosquez

CONTENTS

DEDICATION

To the living God who has given me a life with the heart and
desire to live it.

ACKNOWLEDGMENTS

I would like to acknowledge Jesus Christ as my Lord and Savior through whom I have been given the opportunity, skill and ability to tackle a new life endeavor as an author.

Also, I would like to acknowledge three people who helped me get my first book 'Killing Suicide' off the ground.

Firstly, to Mike Sansone, for being a willing servant of Jesus Christ, my writing coach, friend and conversationalist.

Secondly, to Amanda Browning, for her editing skills, encouragement and help in keeping my voice in my book through her informed editing.

Thirdly, to Christy Baldwin, a lifelong family friend and acquaintance who has become a personal friend and co-worker, who shares similar interests in researching 'success' and who through our weekly luncheons has started and provided an outlet that allows me to see a newer, younger perspective on the world today and how I may be able to help the next generation by sharing my life experiences.

Thank you one and all.

PREFACE

My Mission: To kill suicide. To expose it for the lie that it is. To help those battling with it!

My Purpose: Is to witness to the fact that depression is a symptom of being separated from God.

It is this separation that causes the utter darkness that we feel.

It is these feelings of darkness that make us feel alone, invisible and shrouds our thinking.

It is our darkened thinking which causes the spiraling thought process of depression, the word itself explains where we are...

in a pit of the blackest despair!

This despair in turn, leads many, too many, to take their lives.

FOREWARD

"From family friend, to co-worker, to Godly mentor, Dave has always been around in my life, ever since I was a baby.
33 years later, we connected through work and started having weekly luncheons.
He has helped me re-discover and strengthen my relationship with God. Our weekly luncheons have led to him asking me to read a rough draft of his very first book! I was honored!
Upon reading it, I could not believe it, Dave, a guy I have known my entire life had struggled with depression! And believe it or not, I was actually relieved, because I have struggled with it myself.
In the past few years, I have had a lot of the same feelings.
I now know someone I can relate to and talk to about it. He doesn't look down on me or make me feel ashamed because of it.
After finishing the book, I was confident that I am not the only one struggling with depression. I am certain my depression will not leave on its own.
It will leave by continuing to walk with God.
I know that with my continued luncheons with Dave and my growing walk with God, that I too, will eventually understand true joy!"

Christie Baldwin

Bible Research

The Bible explains that the Darkness comes first.

"Now the earth was formless and empty, darkness was over the surface of the deep, and the Spirit of God was hovering over the waters."
~ Genesis 1:2

"And there was evening, and there was morning - the first day."
~ Genesis 1:5

My darkness was always with me.
As it is with people who suffer from depression, it can become a lifelong affliction.
I am so grateful to God for removing the darkness and showing me the light that I do not have good enough words to describe the joy I now have.
Thank You, Lord.

The darkness has a purpose to it, we can't understand always, but it does.

What would I have to compare the light with if not for the darkness?

"And God said, "Let there be light"... because there already was darkness.
~ Genesis 1:3

When I became a father I was so happy. I wanted to be a dad in the worse way. I couldn't wait to take my kid's fishing, hunting and trapping and to teach them how to read, to teach them to be nice to folks, to teach them to help their grandmas and grandpas.

And when my oldest son was born it hit me... HARD!
I did not want any of my crap splashing up onto any of my kid's. When you grow up in Wisconsin around barns and cows, you know what I'm talking about.

I wish I could say I was perfect in that regard but I wasn't.
I was trying though. I even moved out of my home town so that when my kid's went to school they didn't have any family baggage waiting at the door for them. That worked.

They were able to create lives and identities for themselves based on their own character and actions in school and so in that regard my efforts paid off.

I always had a foreboding feeling when I would think of my past coming into my kid's lives and wreaking havoc, but I did not know where it came from. I just knew that to the best of my ability I couldn't let it in.

I found the 'why' when I was doing research for this book. I found it in the book of Numbers chapter fourteen verses twenty through thirty eight.

It explains how as parents if we do not reconcile with God and change our ways our ways will follow and eventually consume our kid's.

As you see I didn't say, "learn right or wrong".

Another thing I learned creating this book is that it really isn't about right or wrong.

It is about God's ways and our ways, you can label it if you want to but all you'll end up doing is not coming to grips with the facts of the matter.
 In the book of Numbers God is talking to the generation that spoke a bad report to the Israelite community and who rebelled against Him in the desert over and over again to the point of Him, not allowing them, to enter the Promised Land.

Here is how He explains it.

"29 In this wilderness your bodies will fall — every one of you twenty years old or more who was counted in the census and who has grumbled against me. 30 Not one of you will enter the land I swore with uplifted hand to make your home, except Caleb son of Jephunneh and Joshua son of Nun. 31 As for your children that you said would be taken as plunder, I will bring them in to enjoy the land you have rejected. 32 But as for you, your bodies will fall in this wilderness. 33 Your children will be shepherds here for forty years, suffering for your unfaithfulness, until the last of your bodies lies in the wilderness."
~ Numbers 14:29-33

So there it is. My worst fear. My actions could spell disaster for my kids.

My unfaithfulness… causing my kids to suffer.

Even though I suffered with the darkness of depression I was trying to do right by my family and having some good days, and some bad days, and some really, really bad days.

Until, God turned the light on.

Bible research from biblestudytools.com

Baker's Evangelical Dictionary of Biblical Theology - Darkness
"Darkness in both the Old Testament (Heb. hasak [J;v'j]) and
New Testament (Gk.skotos [skovto"]) is an evocative word.
If light symbolizes God, darkness connotes everything that is
anti-God:
the wicked (Prov 2:13-14; 1 Thess 5:4-7)
judgment (Exod 10:21; Matt 25:30)
and death (Psalm 88:12)

Salvation brings light to those in darkness. Although darkness
is opaque to man, it is transparent to God *(Psalm 139:12)*.
Indeed, God can veil himself in darkness at moments of great
revelation,
(Deut 4:11; 5:23; Psalm 18:11).
The biblical view of darkness and light offers a unique
contrast.
There is no thought that darkness is equal in power to God's
light.
The absolute, sovereign God rules over the darkness and the
powers of evil. This is evident in several ways.
First, God knows the darkness.
He knows where it is *(Job 34:22)* and what it contains
(Dan 2:22).
Second, God rules over the darkness because he created it.
(Isa 45:7; Amos 4:13; 5:8)
Third, God uses the darkness for his own purposes:
to hide himself from the sight of men
(Psalm 18:11; 1 Kings 8:12)
and to bring his judgment on evildoers
(Deut 28:28-29; Matt 8:12; 22:13)
 evil nations *(Eze 30:18-19)*, and false prophets
(Jer 23:12; Micah 3:6; Rev 16:10)
Finally, God rules over the darkness eschatologically.

The time of God's ultimate judgment, the day of the Lord, is portrayed in both the Old Testament and New Testament as a day of darkness. *(Joel 2:2; Amos 5:18; Amos 5:20; Zeph 1:15; Matt 24:29; Rev 6:12-17)*

It is against this background that the emphasis on darkness in the crucifixion scene may be understood.
Luke records, *"it was now about the sixth hour, and darkness came over the whole land until the ninth hour, for the sun stopped shining. And the curtain of the temple was torn in two."*
(Luke 23:44-45; Matt 27:45; Mark 15:33).

While darkness often accompanies the conception of death in Scripture *(Job 10:21-22)*, darkness at the crucifixion scene displays God's displeasure on humankind for crucifying his son.
It also indicates God's judgment on evil.
But the torn curtain exhibits the opening of salvation to all through the death of God's Son.
The Old Testament and New Testament describe the future of the ungodly in terms of eschatological darkness, symbolizing perdition *(1 Sam 2:9; Matt 22:13; Jude 12-13).*
"Hell" and "pits of darkness" describe the fate of angels who sinned *(2 Peter 2:4; Jude 6).*
But for believers darkness will be dispelled by the presence of the light of the glory of God
(Rev 21:23-24; 22:5).
It is only through the light of God in Jesus Christ that darkness can be dispelled."
~Michael J. Wilkins

Here is a new thought and action for you, from God's word.
"Turn to me and be saved, all you ends of the earth; for I am God, and there is no other."
~ Isaiah 45:22

Depression Research/Where does it come from?

The Bible explains where depression comes from.

"Anxiety in the heart of man causes depression,"
~ Proverbs 12:25

"Sad hurts but it's a healthy feeling. It is a necessary thing to feel. Depression is very different."
~J.K. Rowling

When I talk to people now about depression, I think some are uncomfortable with it, I know they are, and they say, "Yea, I get sad sometimes too."
I have to look them in the eye and say, "It's not like my dog died!" That's sad.
This is different, very different.
I like J.K. Rowling's quote because I don't think most people understand the difference between sad and a depression that just hangs on and hurts so bad it makes you think the only way you can shut your mind off is to kill it.

Using Strong's word lexicon I looked up the Greek word for anxiety.
Strong's Greek is merimnao' - "a part, as opposed to the whole"
Or properly - "drawn in opposite directions", "divided into parts", figuratively "to go to pieces".
It's an old verb for worry, literally, to be divided, distracted.

Imagine yourself taking apart an orange, dividing the parts, pulling, twisting, and making a mess!
That is exactly what depression is and does to a person, a separation, it separates us.

It separates us from God, from our families, friends. It separates us from a life that could be joyful, productive and clear minded.

It hurts so bad we can see no other way out and so we contemplate suicide as an option.

Because… we just don't know what else to do.

Why? Because we don't believe in a sinful nature, we hear about it but don't really want to believe that could be a cause.

"But your iniquities have separated you from your God;"
~ Isaiah 59:2

The Book of Amos gives us an explanation as to 'the why'.
In *Amos 8:11* it describes a *"famine of hearing the words of the Lord."*

I am writing this book from the perspective of one who is convinced that the sins of the fathers are being visited upon the sons and daughters of today.

As with a 401K account and it gathering interest to pay out a dividend, so are the sins of the fathers if not checked will compound exponentially, generation upon generation, and will have a payment come due whether you believe or not, God does not allow sin to continue on, unchecked forever.

Just ask the Canaanites, Hittites, Amorites and Hivites.

We are killing our own kid's by not dealing with our own depression and our own separation from God.

Maybe with us the gap between us and God wasn't so wide, maybe we had a Grandma who lived out the Word and who knew Jesus, but we refused him, and now because we did not get to know him and live out a relationship with him, for our kid's it has become a great chasm and they are falling into it.

Depression Research
Suffering what is common to man.

I can attest to the fact of not hearing God's word.
I can attest to the fact God has my attention now.
I can attest to the fact he wants me to write this book for you.

I see you. I know your struggle. It's real. God knows it is.

Depression is a truth.
This book is to expose suicide for the lie that it is.

"Take no part in the unfruitful works of darkness, but instead expose them."
Ephesians 5:11

"Until you've had depression I don't think you're qualified to talk about it."
~ Geoffrey Boycott

If you Google depression you will be amazed at the information out there. I was.
Try brainyquotes.com, salon.com, Wikipedia, mentalfloss.com, and smosh.com, along with many, many others.
I was also surprised by the multitude of people who have suffered with it throughout history. Abraham Lincoln, Georgia O'Keefe, Sigmund Freud, William Tecumseh Sherman, even... Siddhartha Gautama, who became 'The Buddha'...
and myself, and you, your cousin, the neighbor kid next door, your Grandma, the Mayor and... and... and...
Terry Bradshaw, Marlon Brando, Johnny Carson and...
Winston Churchill, who famously called his depression, "my black dog."

I watched a PBS documentary on Lewis and Clark and was shocked to learn how Meriwether Lewis suffered from depression and committed suicide, with two pistols, after the expedition. How did I miss that piece of information growing up?

Some of us use the term 'mental illness' for the darkness that our depression causes. If you find... a specific name for your depression... a doctor or two who help you identify it... and they prescribe a course of action for it that helps you...
then you can you use the term 'mental illness'.

A person who does not suffer with it or who suffers with it and has found no help, as was my case, can only call it 'depression'. That's what I'm here to do, call it what it is and talk about it. And to let you know you are not alone... or invisible... or crazy, truth is it may be a severe spiritual attack, carried out by unclean spirits.

Now, don't go and throw the book away!
(Like I would have back in the day.)

I know you may not be ready to hear that, but I'm here to tell you the truth.

If you have looked and looked, like so many do, going to the doctor and trying to determine the cause of your condition and finding nothing, with all the medical information out there today... what else could it be?

Depression Experienced/My Depression Ch. 1

The path of my life, to me, seemed to be just that, a little path, like in the woods, a small and narrow way, with bends, low hanging limbs, raspberry thorns and confusing signs of my times.
Being afflicted with depression is a common malady, so common that some people toss it, and the people who claim to have it, aside with either a wrinkled up nose of distaste or a flippant "just get some happy pill's" remark. It makes the one afflicted even more conflicted about who they are and what is happening to them.

Let me say right now being afflicted with depression is no joke.

My depression was of the constant variety, hidden during the day but would lash out at me at night especially after the age of thirteen when I started using alcohol.
Now, alcohol is quite the liar too. Yes, you can have fun with it. But sooner or later his true colors will come out. So when I found, at first, that alcohol would help hide my depression by allowing me to be the wild kid, the fun kid, the do anything crazy kid... well I rode that bus to and through every scheduled stop!
It worked, for a while, but the inevitable occurred. I fell for the lie that I could handle it...

And from the very first time I consumed alcohol... I was lost to it.

So then my depression became a part of me, throughout my whole life. It stalked me and grabbed me from my path continually.

Through middle school, through high school, through marriage and having kids and still I could not shake it.
No matter what I did.
I took the happy pills, nothin. I tried to be successful, nothin. I tried to just ignore it, nothin. And at certain times it created such a pain, so deep within me, all I could think to do was to kill myself. 'Suicide'

The first time that I seriously considered it I was eighteen or nineteen. I had been out very late drinking with my buddies and when we were done I stayed on the road and headed for my girlfriend's apartment.
My depression wouldn't hit me all at once. It was a gradual thought process that would just slowly spiral down into the dark pit created in my stomach.
All the guilt, pain, loss and discouragement in my life would froth up like the angry foam of a poorly poured beer.

And like so much foam, it would just get poured out... onto my very soul.

So there I was, on the highway at 4:30 a.m. and it started. I was about ten minutes away from my girlfriend's apartment and the highway was devoid of traffic when the voice started.
It was in my head telling me how everything would be better if I was just gone, "Just do it."
I started thinking about semi-trucks and how the driver usually isn't hurt in a crash. I figured the next truck coming at me would be the one. And there was absolutely no traffic on the highway at the time... none.

Then there it was... a lone semi heading my way. Just him and me, I became concerned for the driver so I figured instead of a head on collision; I would just aim for his trailer tires...

The AHA! Moment

Once God raised me up from my depression I was able to take a look around at things and myself.
I looked at myself and had a realization. I didn't know what being a man was.
I just knew I didn't feel like one.

"How can a young man keep his way pure? By living according to your word."
~ Psalm 119:9

"An honest man with an open Bible and a pad and pencil is sure to find out what is wrong with him very quickly."
~ A.W. Tozer

I wanted to know if there was a way I could become a man.
So, I did what I do. I started reading and researching, to find out.
I was led to a website http://www.artofmanliness.com/, created by Brett and Kate McKay, they would get me started. Most of the online community remarks about this site, tote it as 'the' site for manliness. I would have to concur, but there are many, many more out there.
They all point to the fact that I am not alone on this quest to discover what manhood means today.

I was also searching for 'what is success' at the same time.
So, I did what I do. I started reading and researching to find out.
I learned some things along the way about 'success' like, how to utilize a schedule more fully, and how important our health is to our overall being and started to implement those 'successful steps' into my life.

God then showed me my, "what I want to be when I grow up", my very life endeavor.

A WRITER. Whoohoo!

God had placed a man in my life that was willing to help get me started as a writer by building me a website, davebosquez.com and being my writing coach and friend.

As I posted articles to my website, davebosquez.com, a topic came up, my struggle with depression and suicidal thoughts and actions. Being an aspiring writer, I wrote about it.
And doing what I do. I started reading and researching it. Then it became very clear!
I am not alone in a missing manhood, and neither am I alone in my affliction of depression.
It is epidemic. It crosses all lines of men, women, and kid's, and all colors, creeds and nationalities.

Check these sites out, and more, if you don't believe that I am not alone in a missing manhood.
blog.dudepins.com/the-top-10-mens-websites-for-guys/
http://thebachelorguy.com/?dudepins
http://modernmalelifestyle.com/?dudepins
http://brotips.com/?dudepins
http://www.groominglounge.com/
http://urbandaddy.com/?dudepins
http://guymanningham.com/
http://mademen.com/?dudepins
http://gq.com/?dudepins
http://askmen.com/?dudepins
http://artofmanliness.com/?dudepins
The definition of what a man is, is vague, be careful researching manly sites, as with anything on the internet these days.

Depression Experienced/My Depression Ch. 2

The highway I was on, a two lane main artery running east and west across the state went right through the town where my girlfriend's apartment was located.
The plan was to yank the car to the left, under the tires of the semi, and end it all.
My bouts with depression were more like sparring with Mike Tyson.
I never put up much of a fight.
I never understood what kind of hold it had on me and why I would just let it run all over me. The alcohol never helped. It just removed any kind of barrier I may have had and so I would end up a blubbering mess. Some would say the alcohol was revealing the truth.
It would be no different in the car this morning.
I was very emotional, drunk, but not blacked out drunk. Crying drunk... and mad!
I was very aware of what was going on. And I was not imagining the voice in my head encouraging me to "Just do it." "Nobody care's anyway, who cares." "Just do it."
I believed it.
Because when you are in that position, the lies look like the truth.
Because who really cares, right?

"For everyone looks out for their own interests, not those of Jesus Christ."
~Philippians 2:21

The semi was getting close enough now and I started to line it up. I did not move over just yet. I did not want the truck driver to see me coming and move out of the way.
Here it is, The Rubicon, the point of no return.

As I committed in my mind to veer left, at that exact instant a different voice spoke up.
The other voice said, "What will your mom say?"

Did you ever break out in a cold sweat? Well I did. Like when you nod off at the wheel, after working a twelve hour shift, four days straight. Your head nods a bit and you snatch awake, grab the wheel freaking out and instantly sweating, just at your hair line, on the top of your forehead... big cold beads.
It scared me sober. I gripped the wheel very tightly, and pushing myself back into my seat I said, "What?" and the other voice said, "What would your mom think?"

Clear as a bell! I heard that. On my insides I heard that! I did not know God at the time. I knew of him. I had heard of Jesus, who hasn't? But I did not know them at all. I assumed it was God. I didn't know for sure but I knew it scared me sober.

There I was sweating. Then I was mad at myself for being so stupid. How could I put my mom through that? Mad at myself for not doing it, considering myself a coward.
Mad at myself just all the way around. Just mad!!
What a mess I was.
You would think that would be enough to scare anyone into getting help or talking to someone or admitting your problems.
It didn't.

And so, I would continue to deal with my depression, well into my forties.

The Lesson Taught was Separation from God

Separation from God will be, and is, the cause of our darkness. We are dead in our trespasses and sins. All other experiences are just symptoms of being separated.

"Behold, My servants will shout joyfully with a glad heart, But you will cry out with a heavy heart, And you will wail with a broken spirit."
~ Isaiah 65:14

God has revealed to me part of the 'why?' of my past path.
It is to help you, the reader of this message. To understand the darkness you feel, feeling invisible, contemplation of suicide... or worse, attempted suicide...
all are notices of being separated from God.

Pain is a gift from God that tells us when something is wrong. If we get a small pebble in our shoe and it hurts our foot, we don't ignore it all day. We stop, take our shoe off and remove the pebble.
We take notice and take action to relieve the pain.
I am here to tell you this. The darkness can be felt and is felt by more of us than what we have reported. I am here to tell you your darkness is real.
I am also here to tell you that Jesus is also real.
You can continue on, 'having lost all sensitivity', or you can stop, take a small action and remove the pebble from your shoe before it's too late.

"For this people's heart has become calloused; they hardly hear with their ears, and they have closed their eyes. Otherwise they might see with their eyes, hear with their ears, understand with their hearts and turn, and I would heal them.'" ~ Matthew 13:15

I felt hemmed in at times on my little path, but my path did broaden out, maybe not my horizons, but my path broadened and led to marriage, kid's and God himself.

My depression came along for the ride and although it wasn't driving anymore, it would wedge itself up in the front seat, with a regular predictability, and with a sharp elbow to the ribs.

God revealed himself to me when my oldest son was two months old. I followed Him as best as I could. God I mean. Learning things and then forgetting them. Going to church, but not really being a part of it. Having my kid's go through the classes and serve as altar boys.

And my depression persisted.

My drinking slowed down but my depression clung on, like a Bounce dryer sheet, clinging to a pair of your best black trousers, and inevitably I would succeed... in failing.

It was the same pattern, go out and have one, no problem. Next time out, maybe two, what fun! The third time's a charm as they say. So I would go from two drinks to thirty inside a month and the ensuing guilt would start the downward spiraling thought process and I would be gripped with the same thought again and again.

"Kill yourself! It's the answer."

I started to get to know God and believed you can have a personal relationship with Jesus, the Holy Spirit and God the Father, so I just couldn't believe those thoughts in my head anymore.

The spiritual battle had spilled over into my conscience mind and I did not understand what was happening or that the fog I was in was really, spiritual 'battle smoke'.

Over time I came to know the Bible and was listening to different pastors on the radio. One man's name kept being referred to by all those other radio pastors.

Charles H. Spurgeon
Born: June 19, 1834, Kelvedon, United Kingdom
Died: January 31, 1892, Menton, France
"Charles Haddon Spurgeon was an English Particular Baptist preacher. Spurgeon remains highly influential among Christians of various denominations, among whom he is known as the "Prince of Preachers". ~ Wikipedia

If you have not read any of Mr. Spurgeon's articles or sermons I highly recommend you do. I came to know Mr. Spurgeon and read in his biography that he battled depression his entire life. That really struck me. When you read his stuff you can feel that this gentleman really knew God. I didn't understand how someone who lived with God like he did could still suffer from such an affliction. I have come to regard Mr. Spurgeon as one of my teachers. I can type in any bible question to his archives and he will have written a very detailed sermon on that very specific topic. It's marvelous.

God has taught me, that people are given different gifts. Being afflicted is a gift. He places us in the furnace of affliction. He let me experience the darkness and made me aware of it by making me alive.

It's a hard concept to understand, the furnace of affliction. Think of it in the context of a master Japanese swordsmith, who watches intently as the fire and heat start to affect the metal being used, and at just the right time the master swordsmith removes the metal from the furnace and starts the process of shaping and sharpening the instrument according to his desire.

Which as we all know requires a lot of hammering and grinding to boot to get to the finished product.

My depression episodes became moments when I would be closer to God than at any other time. Being in the dark, darkness so heavy you could feel it and yet, aware of His presence.
I would plead for Him to fix me. "Please God!"
I would plead for the strength to ward off the oncoming pattern of behaviors.

To no avail for a lot of years... or so I thought.

Symptoms Stat!

Suicide rates have shown a sharp increase in men from the ages of 45 - 64, in the last 30 years. What may have happened in the last thirty years to cause a spike in the suicide rate among men? I believe, it's because, in the last 30 years individuals of this age group have become men.
Thirty years ago I was 17. Since then I have become a man. One who does not know what a man is, what a man does, how a man needs to act, searching out information to help me gain some kind of a sense of myself after coming out of the proverbial wilderness that I was brought up in.

I was constantly searching for success, respect and love.

The bible says, *"What a person desires is unfailing love;"* *~Proverbs 19:22*

We just do not know what true; Godly love is, in this fallen, sinfully scabbed over world that we live in.

The American Foundation for Suicide Prevention indicates:
7 out of 10 suicides are white males; highest rate of instance is in men aged 45-64.
An article at www.nytimes.com reads, "suicide rate surges to a 30 year high"
"middle age men rose 43%... sharpest increase for males of any age."
The National Center for Health Statistics indicates:
Suicide rates rose 24% from 1999 - 2014 with men and women aged 45 -64 having the sharpest increase.
The information out there is pretty clear, suicide effects all ages, all creeds, all colors and the last 30 years has seen a sharp increase.

I am not here to debate any particular set of numbers, but would like to point out and use the men my age as the topic of discussion. You could say that there are multiple factors for the marked increase in the last 30 years of men committing suicide and struggling with depression.
Mine are not clinical findings.
Mine are a personal experience and a revelation from God.

What is one thing that has happened to every male in the last 30 to 35 years?
He has grown into MANHOOD, and doesn't know what to do with it!
What this lost generation has experienced spiritually is:
a famine of the word of God, hearing and understanding.

"The days are coming," declares the Sovereign LORD, "when I will send a famine through the land-- not a famine of food or a thirst for water, but a famine of hearing the words of the LORD.
~ New International Version Amos 8:11

We have a whole generation of men who do not know how to be the Godly leader of their family. We really have no clue on the responsibilities of a man as God has designed them.
We do not know how to be a husband.
(look up divorce rates, or better yet, those living together but not getting married)
We do not know how to be fathers to our kid's.
("Fifteen million U.S. children, or 1 in 3, live without a father," ~The Washington Times)
We do not know how to take a place of service within our communities. (Check out your local Lions Club membership)

"in the assembly at the gate he has nothing to say",
~ Proverbs 24:7

We expect everything to just work out, blindly blaming anything that doesn't go our way as, "not our fault." We grew up in the age and culture of, Sex and Drugs and Rock 'n Roll!
And alcohol came into the house through ever increasing effective t.v. commercials.
With the statement, "If it feels good do it", as the common cultural mantra.

God does say, "*a famine of hearing the word...*"

Though He still sends his word, "*like the rain and snow that fall from heaven*", He still has people out there preaching. The bible is still the best-selling book in America.

I found this on www.thinkaboutit.com
"The Bible is often said to be the world's best sold book but search the best seller lists and you won't find it anywhere, top to bottom.
It makes you wonder. If it's a best seller why isn't it on the list? Well, the answer is simple.
The annual sales figures for the Bible are so high, averaging between $425m and $650m, repeatedly – year after year – that it dwarfs the sales of all other books. The best any other book can hope for is second place and a very distant second place at that."

My personal search for my manhood and success would lead me into a closer relationship with God the Father and I've come to know Jesus as my King, Master and Brother.
I've also had the pleasure of getting to know the Holy Spirit.
Coming into the Presence of God, he revealed my life's endeavor and my spiritual witness.
We as believers are all called to believe in and witness to His son Jesus of Nazareth, who was put to death on a cross for the remission of sin.

And if we are given a clearer specific message, we are to witness to the other message as well, obediently and boldly.

My witness is to the darkness, experienced by way of a severe depression and suicidal thoughts and actions.

A darkness that I have been made aware of, a darkness that others are suffering with, have suffered with and continue to suffer with. A darkness that God has revealed to me is the darkness that separates us from Him and will utterly separate us from Him on The Day of The Lord.

God wants me to witness to this fact, and it has me scared for those suffering with being separated from Him, scared that they may never be joined with Him.

I have an urgent need to talk to you about this.

This is for you, I see you, and God see's you!

In His Word, God squarely places, the responsibility of knowing, living and passing along His word, on the shoulders of the fathers, the men, of all generations.

I believe today, the sins of our fathers are being visited upon their son's to the third and fourth generations.

Just look at the rampant onslaught of drug use, alcoholism, pornography and suicide, not only of men my age but of our children, kids are second in line for the sharpest increase in suicides and suicide attempts. Kids!

We are killing our kid's! Just because we don't believe in God or His ways doesn't excuse us from the truth of the matter.

As men, we have to stand in the gap, if for no other reason than to protect our kids!

Depression Experienced/My Depression Ch. 4

Then it happened. The same pattern, the same loss of control, thinking I was in control.

Thinking everything was OK but after a near miss of having a physical altercation... I left.

And, as I had come to do over the years, I started walking. I can walk a long way and I can be mad a long time. And I did, and I was.

This walk happened in the middle of a national forest on a two lane highway with no lights. No moon. No stars, the blackest of nights, if ever there was one.

I cannot begin to describe the blackness that I was in both spiritually and physically.

The only light I could make out was each step on the reflecting white line, on the side of the road; it would light up under my foot, splashing, like when you step in a puddle. I even looked up to the sky to see if there was any light that would be causing that to happen.

I chalked it up to being drunk.

I just followed the white line till I blacked out. I didn't come to until about ten miles later. I know it was ten miles because the road I was on ran for seven miles in the direction I was headed and ended when it intersected a county highway. I was well beyond that intersection when I sobered up enough to realize where I was.

I started talking to God. Mad, for the umpteenth time, listening to the deer I would scare, snort and then bound off of the road.

Putting my pocket knife to my throat as I was walking, trying to work up the courage to finally just end it all.

Just walk into the woods and bleed out.

And then there was a bear.

I can't describe the darkness;
I couldn't see my hand in front of my face...
even with my hand touching my face, much less a black bear.
I'm pretty sure it was a bear because of the growl. I stomped
at it and yelled, "HEY! GET OUTTA HERE BEAR!"

It left, I heard it go.

Then...
I heard it come back with a short charge, two or three steps,
heavy steps, crunching the grass, and with a low, "grrhuff."
I went at it again, this time kicking gravel towards the huff
noise. I cannot begin to describe, well enough, the blackness of
that night. PITCH BLACK!

After the bear incident, I was really angry. I started yelling at
God.
I could not understand how he could allow such a thing in a
person's life. I told him how I tried and tried, but couldn't do
anything about it.

Over the years I had contemplated suicide more and more as
an option. Something would always stop me and I would
chalk it up to being a coward.
I would replay the pattern over and over in my mind. I would
pray for him to remove it. I would pray and explain to Him
how I did not believe that this was His will for me, that I knew
what I was thinking was wrong thinking.

I yelled at Him, while pressing my little pocket knife into the
side of my throat,

"YOU HAVE TO DO SOMETHING!"

My Experiences That Show Separation From God

Causes for adult long-term depression, especially in men, are many and varied, but shockingly the same. I had suffered with and through multiple experiences growing up.
As I'm sure you have.

Here's a list.

Childhood sexual abuse: victim at the age of six; and being groomed by an adult work supervisor when I was thirteen.
Being bullied and beaten up by older kids, especially on the bus to elementary school.
Feeling utterly helpless, when I knew the bus driver could see it happening and not do anything to help. I would even miss the school bus on purpose so I wouldn't go through that.
I was described as, "the kid who got picked on more than the kid who crapped his pants."
Alcohol abuse starting at the age of thirteen.
Other addictive tendencies, like drug use.
Reckless risk taking, putting my own and others safety in jeopardy.
Poor school attendance, my mom would say, "Those teachers are making you a nervous wreck!"
She didn't realize I was a nervous wreck.
Poverty, debilitating poverty, without some money you are just frozen in place and time.
No religion, spirituality, or even a simple life goal that could help to point me in the right direction.
Having run-ins with the police due to bad choices and poor behavior.
Having suicidal thoughts.

Feeling Invisible to the world and yet scared that someone might find out the truth.

I had to develop a high operating imagination to get through the day and using a nearby park, comic books, t.v. shows and movies I could 'escape', physically and mentally.
Using apathy as a tool to keep people at bay... "Don't care." "Who cares?" "You don't."

Just getting through to tomorrow, even though knowing, tomorrow will not be different or better. Having the old saying, "well, just suffer through it", become a lifestyle.

It seemed like no one cared, it seemed obvious to me at the time that the adults should have seen what was going on, but if no one ever reports anything... I was afraid to, like I was at fault, that helps to perpetuate the cycle; everyone is just too ashamed and scared and doesn't want to say anything.

Parents maybe are too wrapped up in survival themselves or are so selfish that they are oblivious.
And so we are left to feel the shame, responsibility, guilt and anguish!
All are examples of being separated from God.

The kind of pain depression and suicidal thoughts causes is hard to explain to others when people see we are still operating at some level day to day.
Like going to work, "Gotta go ta' work." "I always went to work."

Like that makes it better or it's is used as an excuse somehow.

It just hurts.
Way down deep and makes you want to curl up as small as you can and maybe, just maybe, today will just go away!

Depression Experienced/My Depression Ch. 5

Depression is real and so is God.

Looking up into the black night, yelling as loud as I could, I opened my eyes and there it was, a yellow barricade light, blinking slowly. It would come on for a few seconds at a time then go off for even longer. Blinking so slowly, I thought I had imagined it. I stopped, blinked my eyes and waited. Yep, there it was. A barricade light, blinking verrry slowwwly.

It had a weird timing to it and looked as if it were hovering up in midair.
"A caution light, that actually makes sense right now."

I had driven this road the day before, there was no construction being done. I looked up to God and said, "Ok, I'll walk up to the light and see what's going on."

As I continued on I realized why it looked like it was floating. I was walking up hill.
"It must be at the top of the hill", I said out loud, to no one.
I made it to the light. It was one barricade light at the end of a driveway. And what, to my wondering eye's did appear? Nope. Not reindeer, civilization. I had made it to the river. There is a supper club there, they have a giant bear statue out front and there are homes and cabins in the area. It is about a twenty minute car ride from where I started and about fifteen to twenty miles to the river. I sat down and took a break.
I thanked God.
After watching two vehicles go by I realized I was still angry, so I started walking again.
I never made it back to where I started and ended up walking well over twenty miles before a nice lady pulled over to give me a ride.

A friend of mine, my best friend, drove three hours to pick me up to bring me home. Everyone should have a friend like that. For my walk, I ended up with... a hurt foot, I left my dog behind and my grown kids were worried about where I disappeared to.

I also haven't had a drink or had a bout of depression since that night.

I believe God has removed those afflictions from me because both desires are gone.

I also ended up realizing that God is a big boy and can take us being mad at Him.

We do not have to tip toe around Him. Let it out! Let it all out!

He removed my affliction in such a way that it could only have been Him. He does that for me. He does things that leave me no doubt as to the fact that He is God and He did a thing in my life for me, for His glory, for his namesake.

Now instead of discouragement and despair when I think of my depression, I am filled with joy. I never knew what real joy was until God removed my depression.

Redeemed Unharmed

Men aged 45 - 64 in the last thirty years have had the sharpest spike of suicide and attempted suicide of any group in that time period.

All ages, genders, colors and creeds suffer from an increase suicide rate over the last thirty years. Middle aged white guys first, kids second.

"Evening and morning and at noon, I will complain and murmur, And He will hear my voice. He will redeem my soul in piece from the battle which is against me, for they are many who strive with me."
~ Isaiah 55:18

"He was a loner, and he was troubled, and he was looking for a father."
~ Norman Jewison (Fiddler On the Roof) quote found on yankeegospelgirl.com describing Steve McQueen… and me.

It took a Godly miracle in my life and the Lord himself to open my eye's to what was transpiring. God was revealing to me his truth.

He has raised me up as a witness to the darkness, the utter blackness, of our lives.

I am here to testify to the fact that our depression is a sign of separation from God.

I am here to testify to the fact that our suicidal urges are a sign of separation from God.

I am here to testify to the fact that being separated from God is the black darkness that can be felt in one's life.

I am here to testify to the fact that the day of the Lord will be darkness and not light.

I am here to testify to the fact that separation from God is HORRIBLE!

When you deal with a depression that hurts so bad you can't even get out of bed in the morning, much less enter the fray of battle, you experience a feeling of being slowly sucked down by a quicksand like fog every day.

I am here to testify to the fact that God does use trials and suffering to teach us, to conform us and yes, love us and though when we are separated from Him we do not understand his unfailing love.

It may not seem right to you at this time, or make any sense yet, but when God revealed to me that HE... placed me into that pit of blackness, in order for me to be able to talk to you about it, openly and candidly, it was absolutely freeing to me!

I was redeemed unharmed... even from myself!

Depressions Epilogue

God has a perfectly timed delivery.
Stan Laurel did too.

"If any of you cry at my funeral, I'll never speak to you again."
~Stan Laurel

And Johnny Carson, although Johnny said he just copied Stan.
I wonder who Stan copied.
Dean Martin was the last great, comedic, straight man that I know of, and that requires impeccable timing.

I thought I understood what had transpired with God removing my depression. But God waited for just the right moment, again, to reveal His bigger purpose for me.
As I was reading *John 16:20*, doing research for one of my website posts,

"and ye shall be sorrowful, but your sorrow shall be turned into joy."

He revealed what he does.
"TURNED INTO"!!!!!!!
Turned into joy!

It really dawned on me what God does...
God takes a thing, and turns it into something else completely!
He takes death and turns it into life.
He takes distrust and turns it into faith.
Weakness into strength.
Water into wine.
Darkness into light.

And draws us with a loving kindness from darkness, from death itself, into His wonderful light, joined not separated.

"For you were once darkness, but now you are light in the Lord.
Live as children of light... "
~Ephesians 5:8

I have been anointed with the oil of gladness today. My darkness has been turned into light. That is a miracle. I now, hopefully, can explain to someone the light of Jesus because he has trained me through the darkness, my darkness, I was the darkness, according to His word.
I know the difference now because I have experienced both.
Yes, both are real and can be experienced.
You do not have to succumb to the darkness or despair. I have now experienced both joy AND utter despair and can speak intelligently about both.

In the words, of Dylan Thomas; "Rage, rage against the dying of the light".

To God his glory. Instead of trying to come up with the words to explain where I am and what has happened to me, I will let God's Word do that.

1 Peter 2:7-12

"7 Now to you who believe, this stone is precious.
But to those who do not believe, "The stone the builders rejected
has become the cornerstone,"
8 and, "A stone that causes people to stumble and a rock that makes
them fall."
They stumble because they disobey the message — which is also what
they were destined for.

9 But you are a chosen people, a royal priesthood, a holy nation, God's special possession, that you may declare the praises of him who called you out of darkness into his wonderful light.
10 Once you were not a people, but now you are the people of God; once you had not received mercy, but now you have received mercy.
11 Dear friends, I urge you, as foreigners and exiles, to abstain from sinful desires, which wage war against your soul.
12 Live such good lives among the pagans that, though they accuse you of doing wrong, they may see your good deeds and glorify God on the day he visits us."

Thank you Lord Jesus!

My Message To You

My message of death is true and so my message of life then is also true.

Kid Rock once said, about song writing, while talking about Johnny Cash, "The good ones borrow and the great one's steal." Meaning that Johnny 'borrowed' a song from another artist and then changed the lyrics and had a hit. I've found writers do the same thing. I have developed my own point of view for sure but sometimes someone has already said it or written it a certain way as to be perfect.

Worked for them, works for me.

Life is full of mountains and valleys, and mole hills that get turned into mountains, and giants that if faced... weren't really giants to begin with. If you have a flatline life with no mountains or valleys, then you are dead.

Which brings me back, to almost plagiarizing a movie scene, I have liked since I was a kid. In the Clint Eastwood classic, 'The Outlaw Josey Wales', there is a scene with Josey Wales meeting the Comanche Indian Chief, Ten Bears.

Josey rides up to the Indian encampment very brazenly.

He is there with a message.

"A message of death."

He says, "this message is here in my pistols and there in your rifle's. I came here this way so that you would know that my message of death is true, and so my message of life then is also true."

Ten Bears replies, "You are the Grey Rider, who doesn't make peace with the blue coats, you may go in peace."

Josey's response is awesome, "I reckon not."

So if I haven't said it right out yet, my message is a message of life and death.

My message of death, my depression, the black dragon of my depression, with talons so sharp digging into my heart, causing me to contemplate suicide, was as real as it gets. God has shown me how being separated from Him is that blackness.

Please, don't continue to be separated from God any longer.

I have shared that with you through my writing. I have shared how God has released me from death once I submitted to him. I tapped out to God.
The rule is, if you tap out to God...
Death has to let you go! See the Book of James Chapter 4:7-10.

"7 Submit yourselves, then, to God. Resist the devil, and he will flee from you. 8 Come near to God and he will come near to you. Wash your hands, you sinners, and purify your hearts, you double-minded. 9 Grieve, mourn and wail. Change your laughter to mourning and your joy to gloom.10 Humble yourselves before the Lord, and he will lift you up."
~ James 4:7-10

Like Josey Wales, my message of death is true.
I offer to you now my message of life, which is also true.
A life created by God, through the Holy Spirit with the atoning blood of Jesus Christ.

You have heard it a million times before but maybe this time it will hit home, "Jesus is the way and the truth and the life".

I can testify to that being true.
It is up to you to determine if, "there is iron in my words of death... and life".

ENVOI

A final word.

I did not hear or see any Godly activity in my house while growing up.

Here are a few examples to point this out in my life concerning going to church.

A brother of a very good friend of mine died July 4th weekend 1987 in a car crash.

The ensuing week or two were very emotional and a large group of us friends attended the funeral services. I was lost and felt out of place at the service. I didn't know what to do or how to act in church. I felt ashamed. I felt I was letting my friend and his brother down.

After the funeral was over a whole group of us had a beer party and ended up driving around on a hay wagon out in the country. As the beer started flowing so did the tears and anger from some of us teenage males and the inevitable occurred. A fight broke out.

One of our friends jumped off of the wagon into the ditch while it was moving, and I dove after him. I got him in a choke hold and if it had not have been for my friend who lost his brother yelling in my ear, "Let him go!" I would have choked our other friend completely out.

I was a mess.

I returned home somehow and was sitting on our small front cement porch. Balling like a baby. My mom sat down next to me and I told her how awful I felt that I didn't know how to act at church and how I felt like I let my friends down.

She put her arm around me when I asked, "Why didn't we ever go to church?"

She said, "I didn't think it was important."

Then, I had an experience with my dad, concerning church attendance.
Some old friends of my mom's took us to church when I was nine years old.
The next day I witnessed my dad screaming at my mom about letting us go to church and yelling at her that he didn't want us, "getting all religious!".
And I mean... screaming!
The bible description would be "a fit of rage."
Well guess what, I loved my mom, and so there wouldn't be... no way, I would ever go to church again, because there ain't no way... it was going to be my fault for my dad to scream at my mom like that again. I found out later in life that some siblings of mine continued to go, but I never went back, not until attending the funeral of my friend's brother.

I didn't go to church until I met my wife. She wanted to get married in her family church and we would end up attending that church with our children for a lot of years.

My dad has been deceased for a long time now.
I wonder what he would say now that I have a minister's license, perform weddings, and have a website dedicated to capturing my experiences with God, and just in general like talking to people about God when I get the chance.

I would like to think we would have grown over time and that he would be proud of me.

"Fathers, do not embitter your children, or they will become discouraged."
~ Colossians 3:21

Many of us men come from homes with no dad at all and some of us had fathers who did not prepare us to be men and fathers ourselves.
When does it stop? Who's on deck!?

The law of the harvest is in full bloom and we are certainly reaping a crop of men from what we have sown with our sons.

It is the man's Godly designed responsibility to teach their son's.

In today's world, moms are left alone to do it, grandma's are left alone to do it, and sometimes a well-meaning auntie is left alone to do it.

That is not God's way.

SOURCES

- Bible quotes provided by, NIV bible, Zondervan Publishing.
- Biblestudytools.com
- Strong's Word Lexicon
- Brainyquotes.com
- Salon.com
- Wikipedia
- Mentalfloss.com
- Smosh.com
- Dudepins.com
- The American Foundation for Suicide
- Nytimes.com
- The National Center for Health Statistics
- The Washington Times
- Thinkaboutit.com
- Yankeegospelgirl.com